Landscapes of
FUERTEVENTURA

a countryside guide

Noel Rochford

SUNFLOWER
BOOKS

Dedicated to Roy and Stephen

Revised printing 1994
First published 1989 by
Sunflower Books
12 Kendrick Mews
London SW7 3HG, UK

Copyright ©1989, 1994
Sunflower Books

*Above: a molino;
a molina is shown
on the title page.*

ISBN 1-85691-038-5

Important note to the reader

I have tried to ensure that the descriptions and maps in this book are error-free at press date. The book will be updated, where necessary, whenever future printings permit. It will be very helpful for me to receive your comments (sent in care of the publishers, please) for the updating of future printings. I also rely on those who use this book — especially walkers — to take along a good supply of common sense when they explore. Conditions change fairly rapidly on Fuerteventura, and *storm damage or bulldozing may make a route unsafe at any time.* If the route is not as I outline it here, and your way ahead is not secure, return to the point of departure. *Never attempt to complete a tour or walk under hazardous conditions!* Please read carefully the notes on pages 7 to 13, as well as the introductory comments at the beginning of each tour and walk (regarding road conditions, equipment, grade, distances and time, etc). Explore *safely*, while at the same time respecting the beauty of the countryside.

Photographs by the author
Maps by John Theasby and Pat Underwood
Drawings by Sharon Rochford
Printed and bound in the UK by KPC Group, Ashford, Kent

10 9 8 7 6 5 4 3 2 1

❀ Contents

Betancuria

✿ Preface

Fuerteventura is different from all the other islands in the Canaries. Being the closest to Africa, there's a definite taste of the Sahara about it. The landscape is thirsty, barren and severe. Here peace and quiet prevails. The countryside is lonely but warm, bleak but friendly and, in its own way, beautiful.

In two things this island excels and outdoes all the others in the archipelago: it has the best beaches and the best climate. Beaches are what Fuerteventura is all about; they 'sell' the island to tourists. You'll find mile upon mile of untouched golden sand, great billowing white sand dunes, foaming surf, and quiet turquoise coves. If you're after sea and sun, this is the island for you! Windsurfers, too, are just discovering the perfect winds to enjoy their hobby.

Even though the landscape changes little, it's pleasant to tour Fuerteventura by car, since there's little traffic on the roads. The pace is relaxing and the landscape timeless. The island's beauty spots are tucked away, often out of sight. I hope this new addition to the 'Landscapes' Series will help you find them

And just in case you get tired of the beaches (which is fairly unlikely), or there's an overcast, cool day, there is some walking to be enjoyed on Fuerteventura. You needn't be an inveterate hiker: there are walks to suit all appetites — rambles across the old worn hills, fairly easy mountain ascents, a seaside hike and, for explorers, rocky *barrancos* in which to flounder. Even the picnic spots will help you get better acquainted with the island. There are hidden streams, palm groves, and crystal-clear lagoons just waiting to be discovered. Lobos — the tiny island of 'anthills' — is another world again. It's a charmer.

Fuerteventura is the richest of the islands in Guanche relics (sorry, Gran Canaria). Few people are aware of this.

The island is littered with Guanche settlements — all untouched. Unfortunately, they are also unprotected and crumbling away. Admittedly, most are hard to distinguish or are well off the beaten track; hence I've only covered a couple of these sites in the book.

Tourism, after having side-stepped this island for so many years, has suddenly struck like a bolt of lightning, and the populace is still reeling from the blow. Being reserved in character by nature, they are still very wary of it all — as we all know, tourism brings with it a lot more than money.... So you may not find the Fuerteventurans as open or as friendly as other Canarians. Speaking some Spanish can make a big difference, especially amongst the village folk and those not involved in tourism.

Landscapes of Fuerteventura will, I hope, give you a better insight into this newly-booming tourist mecca.

Acknowledgements

I would like to express my thanks to the following people for their much-appreciated help:

Andrés Valerón Hernandez, and Claudia, from the Patronato de Turismo de Fuerteventura;

Enrique Abascal, for his 'taxi service' and continual offers of help;

Marie Carmen, from the Cabildo library, for searching the entire shelves for me.

Very special thanks to Sr Francisco Navaro Artiles, who gave up hours of his precious time to help with all my queries, as well as chauffeur me around the island; to Sra 'Maruca' Rodriguez for her kindness; and to my sister Sharon for her excellent drawings.

Finally, thanks to my family, friends, and publishers, who always support my work and travels.

Useful books

Bramwell, D and Bramwell, Z *Wild Flowers of the Canary Islands*. London, Stanley Thornes Ltd.

Bramwell, D and Bramwell, Z *Historia Natural de las Islas Canarias*. Editorial Rueda.

Vicente Araña and Juán Carracedo, *Los volcanoes de las Islas Canarias, II: Lanzarote y Fuerteventura* (with English text). Editorial Rueda.

Carlos Javier Taranilla, *Fuerteventura*. Editorial Everest.

Casa Coronel, in La Oliva

Introduction

Getting about on the island

On Fuerteventura one has no choice but to hire a vehicle, if you want to travel about the island independently. The local bus service is far too limited.

Car hire here is expensive, compared with other islands in the Canaries; however, sharing will cut the cost. **Taxis** are also expensive, because you have to travel fairly long distances (for instance, just to reach your resort from the airport). Here again, sharing lessens the blow. Agree on a price before setting out by taxi, and don't be afraid to bargain politely.

Coach tours are easy to arrange and get you to all the tourist points of interest, but never off the beaten track. The **local bus service** is seldom used by tourists, so you'll be something of a curiosity here! The bus drivers are friendly and obliging. If you do get the opportunity, it's worth doing one of the long, slow hauls once! You'll find **transport timetables** on the touring map.

Picnicking

Most tourists come here for the beaches and the peace and quiet. There are enough beautiful beaches on this island to visit a different one each day for a month. Many of them are off the beaten track, and this means taking along a picnic hamper ... if you intend to spend the day there.

Finding other picnic spots, however, is a different story. There are no 'organised' picnic places on Fuerteventura, unlike some of the other Canary Islands. The picnic settings I've suggested are therefore natural beauty spots I've discovered on my walks. My own personal favourite is Lobos.

On page 14 you will find my suggestions for six lovely picnics, together with all the information you need to reach them. *Note that picnic numbers correspond to walk numbers;* thus you can quickly find the general location on the island by referring to the pull-out touring map (where the walks are outlined in white). Most of the spots I've chosen are very easy to reach, and I suggest where you can park (🚌), walking times, and views or setting. Beside the picnic title, you'll also find a map reference: the exact location of the picnic spot is shown on this large-scale *walking* map by the symbol *P*. Some of the picnics are also illustrated; if so, the photograph reference follows the map reference.

Please glance over the comments before you start off on your picnic: if some walking is involved, remember to wear sensible shoes and to **take a sunhat** (☀ = picnic in full sun). It's a good idea to take along a plastic groundsheet as well, in case the ground is damp.

If you are travelling to your picnic by bus, be sure to verify departure times in advance. Although there are timetables in this book, they *do* change from time to time, without prior warning. **If you are travelling to your picnic by** car, be extra vigilant off the main roads.

All picnickers should read the country code on page 13 and go quietly in the countryside. *Buen provecho!*

Touring

Most visitors to Fuerteventura hire a vehicle for all or part of their stay. As it is quite expensive here, it's a good idea to share with friends. Do shop around, while at the same time bearing in mind that cheapest is not always best! Always check your vehicle in advance and point out any existing dents, scratches, etc. Ask for all the conditions and insurance cover in writing, in English. Check to make sure you have a sound spare tyre and all the necessary tools. Be sure to get the office *and the after-hours* telephone numbers of the car hire firm and carry them with you. If you're not 100% happy about the car, don't take it. Finally, make a note of exactly what you're signing for, if you pay by credit card. *Important:* Leave nothing of value in your car, and always lock it. Car theft is on the increase. Park near to other cars, or where you can keep an eye on your vehicle.

The touring notes are brief: they contain little history or information readily available in tourist office leaflets (which you can obtain free of charge). The main tourist centres and towns are not described either, for the same reason. Instead, I concentrate on the 'logistics' of touring: times and distances, road conditions, and seeing places many tourists miss. Most of all I emphasise possibilities for **walking** and **picnicking**. While some of the references to picnics off the beaten track (indicated by the symbol **P** in the touring notes) may not be suitable during a long car tour, you may see a landscape that you would like to explore at leisure another day, when you've more time to stretch your legs.

   The large fold-out touring map is designed to be held out opposite the touring notes and contains all the information you will need outside the towns. The two largest resorts on the island are Corralejo and Jandía, so I have based the drives around these two centres. The best car tour, in my opinion, is Tour 1 — with the Jandía Peninsula tacked on to it. **Town plans** with exits for motorists are on the touring map. Remember to allow plenty of time for **visits**, and to take along **warm clothing** as well as some food and drink, in case you are delayed. The **distances** quoted in the notes are *cumulative* from the departure point. A **key to the symbols** used in the touring notes on pages 15 to 29 is on the touring map.

   All motorists should read the country code on page 13 and go quietly in the countryside. *Buen viaje!*

Walking

Fuerteventura is a large island; however it does not boast a great variety of landscapes. For this reason the walks in this book are *not* distributed all over the island. Instead, I have covered only the more scenic countryside. As you will see, Fuerteventura *does* offer the walker some picturesque corners.

   There are walks in this book for everyone. To choose a walk that appeals to you, you might begin by looking at the touring map inside the back cover. Here you can see at a glance the overall terrain, the roads, and the location of the walks. Flipping through the book, you will see that there is at least one photograph for every walk. Having selected one or two potential excursions from the map and the photographs, turn to the relevant walk. At the top of the page you will find planning information: distance/time, grade, equipment, and how to get there. If the grade and equipment specifications are beyond your scope, don't despair! *There's sometimes a short or alternative version of a walk,* and in most cases these are far less demanding. *If you want a really easy walk, you need look no further than the picnic suggestions on page 14.*

   When you are on your walk, you will find that the text

begins with an introduction to the landscape and then turns to a detailed description of the route. The **large-scale maps** (generally 1:40,000 or 1:50,000) have been annotated to show key landmarks. Times are given for reaching certain points in the walk. **Note: I am a very fit, very fast walker!** So if you are a beginner, or if you prefer a more leisurely pace, a walk may **take you more than twice as long!** The most imporant factor is *consistency* of times, and I suggest that you compare your pace with mine on one or two short walks, before you set off on a long hike. Don't forget to take bus connections into account!

Note that roads and tracks on the walking **maps** correspond to those on the touring map. The **main walk route** is shown by a solid green line, alternative routes by a dashed green line. A **scale** of miles/kilometres is on each map. Below is a key to the symbols used:

🐦	best views	*P*	picnic spot (see page 7)
♣/♁	church, chapel/shrine	✹	danger; danger of vertigo!
◄●	spring, tank, etc	🚗	car parking
□▫□	habitations	■	building in the text
⚡	pylon, wires	▬	walls (usually stone)

The walks in the north can be done using local tranport. Those in the centre of the island require private transport and, accordingly, I have made them circular walks. In the south, the hikes are virtually on your doorstep. No guides are required for any of the walks; you cross open countryside. Climbing Pico de la Zarza, however, needs a cloudless day; otherwise you're asking for trouble. One walk which I have purposely left *out* of the book is the unique stretch of beach from Morro del Jable to Costa Calma (23km; 3h45min *my time, remember*). This needs no explanations, and nearly everyone does some part of it. If you're fit try the whole stretch. What a ramble!

Dogs and other nuisances

The only way **dogs** will bother you is by following you and tripping you up! Goatherds' dogs are all bark and no bite. Usually, where there are goats and sheep, you find **ticks** as well. Fuerteventura is no exception, but because there isn't much long grass they are less of a nuisance here than elsewhere.

Weather

Fuerteventura has a climate to match its beaches: The mean average temperature is 19°C, with fairly hot summer days and a very mild winter ... to say nothing of a healthy 2900+ hours of sunshine per year!

November to March are the best walking months. Sun-seekers, I'm sorry to say that you *will* get cloudy days, some quite miserable and fresh — just right for a long hike. *Wet* days — from the blessed (for the islanders) west- to southwest winds — are quite a phenomenon here; they arrive about as frequently as a *real* summer in England (when everybody remembers the year…).

The main winds are the northeast to north, which can be very strong in spring and summer — just right for wind-surfing, and the bothersome southeast to south — a dry hot wind off the Sahara that fills the air with dust. These winds only last for two to three days, but can be very unpleasant. In summer, mists (from the trade winds) are common over the Jandía mountains, but they won't affect your beach days. So really, all you've got to worry about is the sun and the heat. Don't overdo it on your first day!

Where to stay

There are two main resorts on the island: Corralejo in the north and Jandía in the south. For walkers neither has the advantage over the other. There are also a number of sea-side villages where you can find apartments if you're travelling independently: try El Cotillo, El Castillo, Las Playitas, Tarajalejo, La Lajita, and Ginijinamar. But, as with Puerto del Rosario, finding unreserved accommodation in 'the season' is difficult.

The bus service is better *going to* Puerto del Rosario than travelling *from* it. There is no accommodation speci-fically for tourists in the capital, but don't let that worry you; it is the least attractive and least friendly place on the island. Morro del Jable, Corralejo and Costa Calma are all architectural nightmares … but they do straddle superb beaches.

What to take

If you're already on Fuerteventura when you find this book, and you don't have any special equipment such as walking boots or a rucksack, you can still do some of the walks — or buy yourself some equipment in one of the sports shops. Don't attempt the more difficult walks with-out the proper gear. For each walk in the book, the *mini-mum* equipment is listed.

Please bear in mind that I've not done *every* walk in this book under *all* weather conditions. Use your good judgement to modify my equipment list according to the season!

You may find the following checklist useful:

walking boots (which *must* be broken-in and comfortable)
waterproof rain gear (outside summer months)
long-sleeved shirt (sun protection)
bandages and band-aids
plastic plates, cups, etc
anorak (zip opening)
extra pair of socks
plastic groundsheet
sunhat
insect repellant

up-to-date transport timetables
lightweight water containers
small rucksack
long trousers, tight at the ankles
protective sun cream
knives and openers
2 lightweight cardigans
spare bootlaces
torch
whistle
compass

Spanish for walkers and motorists

In the tourist centres you hardly need know any Spanish at all. But once you are out in the countryside, a few words of the language will be helpful, especially if you lose your way. It may also help you 'break through' the natural reserve of the Fuerteventurans.

Here's an — almost — foolproof way to communicate in Spanish. First, memorise the few short key questions and their possible answers, given below. Then, when you have your 'mini-speech' memorised, always ask the many questions you can concoct from it **in such a way that you get a "sí" (yes) or "no" answer.** *Never* ask an open-ended question such as "Where is the main road?". Instead, ask the question and then *suggest the most likely answer yourself.* For instance: "Good day, sir. Please — where is the path to Cofete? *Is it straight ahead?*" Now, unless you get a "sí" response, try: "*Is it to the left?*" If you go through the list of answers to your own question, you should eventually get a "sí" response!

Following are the most likely situations in which you may have to practice your Spanish. The dots (...) show where you will fill in the name of your destination. Ask a local person — perhaps someone at your hotel — to help you with the pronunciation of place names.

Asking the way
Key questions

English	Spanish	Pronunciation
Good day, sir (madam, miss).	Buenos días, señor (señora, señorita).	**Boo**-eh-nohs **dee**-ahs, sen-**yor** (sen-**yor**-ah, sen-yor-**ee**-tah).
Please — where is	Por favor — dónde está	**Poor** fah-**vor** — **dohn**-day es-**tah**
the road to ...?	la carretera a ...?	lah cah-reh-**teh**-rah ah ...?
the footpath to...?	la senda de ...?	lah **sen**-dah day ...?
the way to ...?	el camino a ...?	el cah-**mee**-noh ah ...?
the bus stop?	la parada?	lah pah-**rah**-dah?
Many thanks.	Muchas gracias.	**Moo**-chas **gra**-thee-ahs.

Possible answers

English	Spanish	Pronunciation
here?	aquí?	ah-**kee**?
there?	allá?	ayl-**yah**?
straight ahead?	todo recto?	**toh**-doh **rayk**-toh?
behind?	detrás?	day-**tras**?
right?	a la derecha?	ah lah day-**ray**-chah?
left?	a la izquierda?	ah lah eeth-kee-**er**-dah?
above?	arriba?	ah-**ree**-bah?
below?	abajo?	ah-**bah**-hoh?

Asking a taxi driver to take you somewhere and return for you, or asking a taxi driver to meet you at a certain place and time

English	Spanish	Pronunciation
Please —	Por favor —	**Poor** fah-**vor** —
take us to …	llévanos a …	l-**yay**-vah-nohs ah…
and return for us at (place) at (time).*	y venga buscarnos a … a … .*	ee **vain**-gah boos-**kar**-nohs ah (place) ah (time).*

*Just point out the time on your watch.

A country code for walkers and motorists

- **Do not light fires.**
- **Do not frighten animals.** The goats and sheep you may encounter on your walks are not tame. By making loud noises, or by trying to touch or photograph the animals, you may cause them to run in fear and be hurt.
- **Walk quietly** through all hamlets and villages.
- **Leave all gates just as you find them.** Although you may not see any animals, the gates *do* have a purpose — generally to keep goats or sheep in (or out of) an area.
- **Protect all wild and cultivated plants.** Don't try to pick wild flowers or uproot saplings. Obviously fruit and other crops are someone's private property and should not be touched. *Never walk over cultivated land.*
- **Take all your litter away with you.**
- **Walkers — *Do not take risks!*** This is the most important point of all. Do not attempt walks beyond your capacity, and do not wander off the paths described here if there is any sign of mist or if it is late in the day. **Do not walk alone** (four is the best walking group), and *always* tell a responsible person *exactly* where you are going and what time you plan to return. Remember, if you become lost or injure yourself, it may be a long time before you are found. On any but a very short walk close to villages, be sure to take a compass, whistle, torch, extra water and warm clothing — as well as some high-energy food, like chocolate. Read and re-read the important note on page 2, as well as guidelines on grade and equipment for each walk you plan to do!

Picnic suggestions

1   LOBOS (map page 31; photograph page 32)

by 🚢: 10-15min on foot. Ferry from El Cotillo to Lobos.
Head left straight off the jetty; less than 10min along, spot a path branching off left, into sand dunes. This leads to lovely Playa de la Calera. If you prefer swimming off rocks, try the stunning setting of Casas El Puertito, 5min from the jetty (to the right). Both are superb, tranquil spots. ✪

2   EL COTILLO (map pages 34-5, photograph page 37)

by 🚗: 5-10min on foot. Park off the side of the lighthouse road, north of El Cotillo.
Picnic at any of the delightful turquoise coves or on the dunes near the lighthouse. ✪

5   BARRANCO DE LAS PEÑITAS (map page 45, photographs pages 25 and 47)

by 🚗: 10-20min on foot. Park beyond the last houses on the Presa de las Peñitas road (south of Vega de Río de Palmas), off curve above reservoir.
Skirt the reservoir to the right to reach the dam wall, and use notes on page 46 to descend (with care) to the chapel, which offers the only shade in this sun-baked setting. ✪

6a   BARRANCO DE LA MADRE DEL AGUA (map page 49, photograph page 51)

by 🚗: 10-15min on foot. Park in Ajuy (9km west of Pajara on the Puerto de la Peña road), just before a roadside house above the barranco.
Enter the bed of the barranco down to your right and walk left along it to the tiny ravine that cuts back off this one, a few minutes along. It's choked with palms and has a lovely little brook with a footbridge. Picnicking in a setting like this is rare indeed on Fuerteventura!

Tree
candelabra

6b   CALETA NEGRA (map page 49)

by 🚗: 15-20min on foot. Park in Puerto de la Peña.
*Follow the old port path out of the village (right). When it ends, climb to the top of the crest above, and continue along the coast. In 3min overlook Caleta Negra. The notes on page 52 tell you how to reach the old port and sea-caves. This descent is only for the **very** sure-footed picnicker!* ✪

8   COFETE (map page 56)

by 🚗 (jeep or 4-wheel drive only): 0-5min on foot. Take the first turnoff left outside Cofete hamlet to the beaches of Cofete and Barlovento de Jandía. Park on the beach.
Picnic anywhere. Note that the sea is very dangerous; treat it with respect. No shade. ✪

Morro del Jable • La Pared • Betancuria • La Antigua • Gran Tarajal • Las Playitas • Morro del Jable

190km/118mi; 5 hours driving; Exit A from Morro del Jable

En route: P5, 6a, 6b; Walks 4, 5, 6, 7

The main north—south road is generally good. However, between La Antigua and Tarajalejo it's rough and full of potholes. Inland roads are good, but narrow. Between Pájara and Vega de Río de Palmas the road is quite high and winding; some people will find this stretch unnerving, since there is not always a roadside barrier. Watch out for animals on the roads in the countryside, and for pedestrians in the villages. Local people seem to drive very fast, so stay alert. Note also that it can be very windy. The only petrol stations en route (closed Sundays and holidays) are in Tuineje and Gran Tarajal.

Opening hours: Museo Sacreo (Betancuria): 10.00-14.30 and 15.30-17.30 daily except Sundays. You can also obtain the key to the cathedral here at the museum.

This drive takes you to some of the best sights on the island, from the most stunning beaches to the most picturesque valleys. You will be treated not only to the beauty spots, but also to the geographical and geological wonders of the island. And the final ingredient to flavour this tour to perfection is the little village of Betancuria — Fuerteventura's ancient capital.

Leaving Morro del Jable we take the GC640 as far north as the junction for La Pared. Out of the eyesore of development, we wind in and out of the deep bare *barrancos* that cleave the mountainous backbone of the Jandía Peninsula. Pico de la Zarza (806m/2645ft), the island's highest summit, can be seen at the end of both the Vinamar and Butihonda valleys. It's a modest peak that rises a mere shoulder above its off-siders. On a fine day, however, you can have a most enjoyable hike here — see Walk 7.

Close on 16km out of Morro del Jable, just as we leave **Barranco Los Canarios** (✕), we round a corner and come to a stunning view over the captivating Playa de Sotavento de Jandía★ — the queen of Fuerteventura's beaches (see pages 17 and 21). A track forks right off the corner here and descends to the beach below. Pull over onto this track, so that you can really appreciate this magnificent coastal vista or, if you want to get closer still, take the track opposite the Restaurante Bei Michael a kilometre further on and follow it towards the sea; you'll end up atop the dunes. The beach widens into an expansive sand bar, and the sea will no doubt be dotted with a myriad of colourful windsurfs. In the background the coastline curves sharply right, and off the beach rise the giant sand hills of the Pared isthmus — through which we are about to pass.

15

Just before we turn off the main road, at the end of the dunes, we pass through **Costa Calma** (25km ▲▲▲✕, another *urbanización* constructed without regard to preserving the beauty of the coast. Some 27km from Morro del Jable, we turn off left for La Pared, at a junction 1.5km beyond Costa Calma (not signposted). After 5km we reach **La Pared** (▲▲▲✕), which sits in a desolate and naked landscape on the outskirts of the dunes. This scattering of buildings looks sad, neglected and unsightly, so let's head on to Pájara. The cloud-catching hills rising on our right, of which Montaña Cardón (691m/2265ft) is the highest, cut off the west coast from the rest of the island. A few kilometres out, we encounter the first of the 'zona militar' signs — all of which are barely discernible. This prohibited area (a firing range) stretches along almost all the way to Pájara, so don't drive onto any tracks or roads branching off towards the coast.

We pass the quiet cultivated valley of Huertas de Chilegua, and the road climbs into smooth rounded hills sparse of vegetation. (The absence of side-railings on this road may make it unnerving for some people.) These ochre-coloured mounds are of the basement complex, ie the oldest hill formations. Descending to another isolated farmstead, you'll see small earthen reservoirs in the valley floor. These are called *presas secas* ('dry reservoirs'), because they have been constructed to catch the water that comes down the *barrancos*, but they do not retain it. The water passes through the permeable soil into wells which have been sunk some 17-20m (about 60ft) below the ground in front of these *presas*. The small metal windmills you see everywhere are used to pump this water up to ground level again (see page 29).

Closer to Pájara the hills open out into a vast depression. Meet a junction (54km) and turn left, to descend to Ajuy/Puerto de la Peña. Rounding a corner, we look down into a valley lush with palm trees, tamarisk shrubs and garden plots. Notice the small ravine crammed with palm trees cutting back off it, into the hills running down on the right. This ravine (*P*6) boasts the only permanently-flowing stream on Fuerteventura. It's only a trickle, but the picnic spot is enchanting (see page 51).

Puerto de la Peña (63km), a small village set on the edge of a black sand beach, is one of two fishing settlements on the west coast. Few tourists venture over to the dramatically-sited ancient port here. It hides in a bay some ten minutes' walk around the coast to the south of the village. I'd suggest you use the notes for *Picnic 6b* to discover the huge sea caverns that open out back off this port ...*but only if you are **extremely** sure-footed.*

From Puerto de la Peña return to the junction and keep straight on to **Pájara** (74km ♣ ✕ and swimming pool). This is a large farming community surrounded by hills. The shady village is a welcoming sight, with its abundance of trees and small colourful gardens. Don't miss the church

Playa de Sotavento de Jandía — Fuerteventura's finest beach

here; it is especially noteworthy for the striking 'Aztec' stone-carved decoration above the main entrance. Quite a curiosity because, apart from a similar lot of sculptures in La Oliva, these carvings are unique in the Canary Islands. The two naves inside the church date back to 1645 and 1687, while the carving over the door is thought to date from the 1500s.

Leaving Pájara take the road for Vega de Río de Palmas; it's at the left of the church. Again we ascend into the hills, climbing on a narrow winding road that hugs the sheer inclines (again, some people might find this road unnerving). There are excellent views back over the Barranco de Pájara. The Degollada de los Granadillos (📷 with parking for *one* car only) is the pass that takes us over a solid spur of rock that juts out into the valley below. It's a dangerous corner for parking! From this pass you have a superb outlook over to the enclosing rocky ridges.

Soon, descending, we look down onto the Presa de las Peñitas, a muddy reservoir lodged in the 'V' of the Barranco de las Peñitas. The reservoir looks deeper than it is; it's only about 1 metre (3ft) deep, since it has filled up with silt. Groves of tamarisk huddle around the tail of the *presa*, and that's a good spot from which to do some bird-watching. Green gardens step the sides of the slopes, and palm trees complement the scene. Below the reservoir lies a sheer-sided rocky ravine, the ideal hiding place for the chapel dedicated to the island's patron saint, Nuestra Señora de la Peña (*P*5). This impressive ravine, one of the island's beauty spots, is well worth exploring; see photographs on page 47.

One of the many valleys that sit concealed in the hills surrounding Pájara; this one lies behind Toto (Car tour 1).

Tour 1: There are some unusual carvings on the façade of the church at Pájara — a mixture of Gothic and Aztec decoration. Other examples of Aztec influence are found at La Oliva (see Tour 3).

Now the rest of the valley opens up, and a string of *casas* stretches along it. They're set amidst a healthy sprinking of palms and cultivated plots — a luxuriant corner (see page 25). The first turn-off you encounter, just before the centre of **Vega de Río de Palmas** (85km) leads down to the reservoir. We continue on the main road by twisting our way up the valley. The countryside subsides into rolling contours once again. Notice a large abandoned field of sisal on the hillsides on your left, a short distance further on. This plant was introduced from Mexico.

At the end of this valley we come to the village of **Betancuria ★** (90km ✝ ♦ ✖M; photograph page 26), well hidden from the marauding Berbers of earlier centuries. It's a very picturesque collection of manorial buildings, with a grand 17th-century cathedral. The cathedral and convent here are the oldest examples of their style in the archipelago. Relics abound in historic Betancuria, and I hope you'll notice some of them. A number of the old houses have doorways and arches dating back to the 15th century. Betancuria was the capital of Fuerteventura for some 400 years, up until 1835, and was also the first episcopal seat for all the Canaries. The oldest part of the village huddles around the church — much of it slowly deteriorating. History-hunters will enjoy the cathedral and the small Museo Sacreo here — as well as the municipal museum. Everyone passes by the Franciscan monastery, the shell of which sits below the road on the northern side of the village. Inside it (unseen from the road) are some beautiful cloistered arches (see sketch page 4). Near the convent is a small enclosed church — actually the first church on the island; however much of the building was rebuilt in the 17th century.

Every rural household seems to have its handful of sheep, goats and fowls. All live together in happy harmony.

We zig-zag up out of the valley, and pull over at the top of the pass for a fine panorama over a vast plain to the north. Its far-distant reaches are edged by sharp abrupt hills called *cuchillos* (knives); over on our left lie *morros* (low, smooth hills). Betancuria nestles cosily in the valley floor below. Leaving the viewpoint, we soon pass the turn-off left to Valle de Santa Inés and Llanos de la Concepción (Walk 4). Another expansive plain stretches out below us now, and La Antigua sits below on the edge of it.

Entering **La Antigua** (100km ✝✗), we come to the beautifully laid-out square, with the simple but neverthe-less imposing church. Just north of La Antigua (on the Puerto del Rosario road) stands El Molino ★ (✗), a well-preserved 200-year-old windmill, once used for grinding corn. The windmill (*molino*) is an appropriate intro-duction to La Antigua, because this area has the highest concentration of windmills on Fuerteventura — as you will see! From here we head south towards Tuineje.

Out in the country again, palms return to the scene. A trickle of villages is seen sitting back in the plain. Threading our way through hills, we find cultivated fields sheltering along the floors of the *barrancos*. **Agua de Bueyes** (106km ✗) is the next village en route. Three dark volcanoes, La Laguna, Liria and Los Arrabales, rupture the lake of lava that spills out over the plains on your left. This area is called the *malpais* ('badlands'). Around **Tuineje** (112km ☎) the large *fincas* of the tomato-growers are a prominent feature in a barren landscape.

Coming into **Gran Tarajal** (125km ☎☎✗⊕), you look out over lean groves of palms dispersed along the valley floor. Tamarisk (*tarajal*) shrubs add to the verdure. This small port and fishing village is second to Puerto del Rosario (and, to me, much more appealing than the capi-tal). The houses step back up the steep sides of the valley and overlook the black sand beach that curves around the mouth of the *barranco*. Some 6km from Gran Tarajal lies the island's prettiest seaside village, **Las Playitas** (131km ▲✕), terracing a rocky hillock which conceals a lovely dark-sand beach stretching out behind it. Curiosity-seekers may enjoy a detour to El Faro de Entallada.

Homeward bound, return to the GC620 and bear right, then left, for Tarajalejo. (Giniginamar — an optional 8.5km return detour ▲✕ — is a small fishing village, set deep in a *barranco*. To reach it, turn off 6.5km from the Gran Tarajal junction.) **Tarajalejo** (152km ▲▲▲✕), once a quiet fishing hamlet, occupies the end of a sweeping beach. Tourism is fast changing all this, as hotels and apartments quickly fill the *barranco* floor. Just over 4km further on, pass a turn-off left for La Lajita, another fishing village all set to capitalise on the tourism boom. We climb amidst low hills, snatching views of pretty coves with not a soul about. Mounting the top of a crest (Cuesta de la Pared, 159km ✕▣), we have a splendid view of Jandía, encompassing the mountains with the identical twin peaks of Zarza (Walk 7) and Mocán, and the luminous blue and green ribbon of beaches that are the fame of Fuerteventura. Shortly, we rejoin our outgoing route, and I'm sure that this unparalleled coastline will draw you down once more to the beach, before the day is out.

This ma-rooned sailing yacht probably never thought it would end its days as a landmark on the Playa de Sotavento — nor did its owner.

Morro del Jable • Jandía • Cofete • Morro del Jable

63km/39mi; 3-4 hours driving; Exit B from Morro del Jable

En route: *P* 8, Walk 8

*From beginning to end we follow an exceptionally rough gravel road —
the worst part being the circuit to Cofete. This drive is really only
recommended for four-wheel drive vehicles, especially the Cofete
stretch! Before venturing off in a hired car, read what your rental
agreement says about travelling on **unsurfaced** roads. Note that there are
no petrol stations (and hardly any people) out here … if you break down!
Also, avoid this route after wet weather. This route appeals to the 'rally
drivers' in the population, so drive carefully and attentively, looking out
for speeding traffic. Note also that the peninsula can be very windy, and
that petrol stations are closed on Sundays and holidays.*

As bleak and unfriendly as this landscape may appear,
it is far from unappealing. The wall of ancient
volcanic mountains that dominates the Jandía Peninsula
harbours severe but striking valleys. An air of loneliness
and calm lingers over the plains. Crossing the *cumbre*
from east to west you have spectacular views: the
mountains become more impressive as they sweep back
up into sheer cliffs, the cast beaches more alluring with
their pounding surf. The east coast harbours a number of
secluded coves, the west coast splendid sweeps of sand.
So if you fancy an 'away from it all' beach day, pack a
healthy picnic and make a day of it.

Punta Jandía/Cofete are best reached via the port road,
which circles above Morro del Jable. We turn off just
above the port onto a (signposted) gravel road forking off
to the right. Heading out into one of the most desolate
corners of the island, we bump our way in and out of small
deep *barrancos*. Nearly all of them terminate in pretty
sandy coves — usually accessible only on foot.

Crossing a vast open plain less than five kilometres out,
we pass a fork-off to the right. It heads up into a wide
valley (Gran Valle) that carves a great gap out of the Jandía
massif. This valley offers an alternative route to Cofete —
on foot! This is the old mule track that was the main
east—west link; walk 8 follows it. *Note:* only about 100
metres up the Gran Valle track lies a magnificent
community of rare *Euphorbia handiense* (see opposite).

Sharp rocky ridges dominate the landscape. Low salt-
resistant vegetation — *cosco, aulaga*, ice plants and
Lycium intricatum are the inhabitants of this intractable
terrain. Goats roam deep in the *barrancos*. The large
tomato plantation of **Casas de Jorós** comes as a surprise
way out here in this semi-desert countryside.

Towards the end of the island the plain broadens, and

the *barrancos* become less significant. The mountain chain breaks up and slowly subsides into disjointed hills. At Punta de Jandía, the tip of this boot-shaped peninsula, stands the lighthouse. Some 12.5km out of Morro del Jable, we come to the turn-off for Cofete (not signposted). Keeping left, first descend to the lighthouse. Tracks branch off to coves ensconced in the low rocky shoreline running along on the left. Approaching the sleepy fishing hamlet of Puerto de la Cruz, we come onto tarred road, which continues on to the lighthouse (*faro*) 2km further on.

  Puerto de la Cruz (21km ✕) seems more like a weekend retreat than a fishing hamlet. Its small adjoining houses sit on the edge of the plain, looking out to sea. **Punta de Jandía** itself is unimpressive; however, you do have a fine view back along the deeply-dissected mountains of the peninsula. Off the point lies an underwater reef called Bajar del Griego ('where the Greek sank'). Some 200 years ago, a Greek ship carrying passengers from Fuerteventura to Gran Canaria hit this reef and sank, with all lives lost.

Tour 2: Only about 100 metres up the Gran Valle track you will see this fine refuge of the rare Euphorbia handiense. Walk 8 follows this old mule track, once the main east—west route across the peninsula.

If you have a four-wheel drive vehicle, now bounce along the track that follows the coast westward, to the pretty rocky cove of Playa de Ojos, some 2km along. Then return to the Cofete turn-off, bear left, and zig-zag up over a pass (⬛ with limited parking). Over the *cumbre* a magnificent vista greets you — one of the very best views on the island: you look straight along the golden beaches of Cofete and Barlovento de Jandía. Together they stretch nearly the length of the peninsula. The white-crested breakers and blue-green sea light up the sombre plain and shadowy summits. In the distance rise the billowing sand dunes of the Pared isthmus. Our road, no more than one lane wide, is carved out of the steep face of the escarpment. It was built to enable a certain Señor Winter to construct his mansion out here (see below). Further down the track, you'll spot a large colony of *cande-labra*, a large multi-armed, cactus-like plant resembling a chandelier. The villagers once used the latex of this plant to catch fish: they put it into rock pools to stun the fish and bring them to the surface.

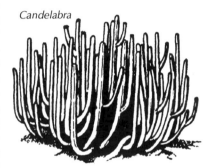

Candelabra

Cofete (40km ✖ *P*8) is a rustic settlement of stone (and more recently, cement) huts and a restaurant. Its simple low dwellings give it the appearance of a Guanche settlement. Señor Winter, the German who owned the peninsula, forbade anyone to live here, so it never grew into a real village. His villa (see page 58 and sketch page 59) is the main feature of the plain.

Pass through Cofete and bear right. After some 200 metres, you'll meet a track forking off to the left. This leads to a never-ending beach. ***Important:*** the beaches here are dangerous at all times. A cross-current runs just off the shore, and a number of tourists have drowned. Enjoy a picnic, perhaps, and a paddle, but please do not swim! The Winter residence (which no longer belongs to the same family) lies another 1.7km away, should your curiosity get the better of you, but even four-wheel drive vehicles struggle over this stretch of track.

Follow the same route back to Morro del Jable.

3 NORTHERN LANDSCAPES

Corralejo • Puerto del Rosario • La Matilla • Los Molinos •Tindaya • La Oliva • El Cotillo • Corralejo

129km/80mi; under 4 hours driving; Exit A from Corralejo

En route: *P*2; Walks 2, 3

Roads are generally good. Country roads are narrow and occasionally bumpy. Watch out for animals on the roadsides and for pedestrians in the village streets. It can be very windy along the coast. Note that there are petrol stations only in Puerto del Rosario and Corralejo (closed Sundays and holidays).

Barranco de las Peñitas — one of the island's most picturesque valleys (Car tour 1; Picnic 5)

The circuit that this tour follows is fascinating rather than 'beautiful'. Impressive hills and volcanoes border the great interior basins of emptiness. During the second half of the tour you wind in and out of a rough sea of lava called the *malpais* — the 'badlands', a curious sight, with its surprising amount of plant life and greenery. And, if you're bored with the sand dunes of Corralejo, then El Cotillo will prove quite a treat, with its cliff-backed beach and dazzling turquoise coves.

Leave Corralejo on the coastal road to Puerto del Rosario (Exit A) and head out through the dunes. This stunning stretch of white shimmering sand is further enhanced by the aquamarine sea and the purply-blue hills that rise up in the background. Lobos (Walk 1) stands out clearly on your left, offshore, with its hundreds of little hillocks and guardian volcano. The dunes are supposedly a natural park, but all the same, two hotels interrupt this unique stretch of beauty (4.5km ▲▲✕).

Tour 1: Betancuria houses a wealth of fine old buildings. This village was the capital of Fuerteventura for some 400 years.

Out of this mini-desert, we cross a featureless stone-littered plain. A number of tourist booklets recommend a detour to Parque Holandés (⬢✕), but I would advise you to skip it. **Puerto del Rosario** (30km ⬢⬢⬢✕✝🔊⊕) has little to offer, being visibly the poorest town on the island. However, at Hostal Macario you'll find good home-cooking.

Beyond Puerto del Rosario, our tour really begins, as we head back northwest to Corralejo via the inland route*. Head straight out of town on Calle León y Castillo (on the right-hand side of the church, Exit B). This takes you onto the GC600. A gentle ascent across a stony plain brings us up to the old airport of Los Estancos, and we cut straight through the centre of it. Entering a grand U-shaped valley, we pass through **Tetir** (38km), a well-spread farming village. The enclosing hills are eroded and rocky, bare of vegetation. Montaña Aceitunal (686m/2250ft) dominates the valley with its sharply-pointed features. Climbing out of this valley, we reach a higher one and come onto the pretty village of **La Matilla** (43km). Another prominent mountain of equal proportions overshadows the village: Montaña Muda (689m/2260ft).

Descending from this basin meet a junction at 45km and bear left. **Tefía** (51km), a sad, forgotten-looking village of decaying stone buildings, sits quite lost in this quiet corner. We turn off down the first road forking off to the right beyond Tefía (signposted for Puertito de los Molinos). Wine-coloured *cosco* patches the arid flat. Pass through the village of **Colonia García Escamez**, a farming settlement built after the construction of the nearby (but out of sight) Embalse de los Molinos. Walk 4 takes you to this *embalse* (reservoir; see photograph page 44). Dip down into the Barranco de los Molinos. It's a pretty valley to explore (downstream), especially after a wet winter, when you'll find a stream and some rock pools. **Los Molinos** (62km) is a tiny fishing hamlet that huddles off a lovely bay encircled by the rock cliffs that open off the mouth of the *barranco*.

Return to the junction below La Matilla and bear left for Corralejo. Rounding a corner, we look over onto the dark sandy volcano of Montaña Quemada. This particular

*An alternative route back to Corralejo lies further south and would take you via El Castillo (⬛⬢⬢ ⬢✕). I don't think this itinerary is worth the extra kilometres. However, if you're making a trip to Jandía, either go or return via this route to see the enormous U-shaped valleys beyond El Castillo. Visit, too, Pozo Negro (⬢✕), an out-of-the-way fishing village sprinkled across a lava tongue — a 17km (return) detour.

volcano is rather special because at its base there is a modest monument dedicated to the famous Spanish poet Unamuno, who lived in exile on Fuerteventura.

We next pass above **Tindaya** (81km ✕). It spreads across a flattened crest amidst a profusion of faded brown stone walls. Behind the village stands captivating Montaña Tindaya (the setting for Walk 3), a great rocky salient that dominates the surrounding countryside with its boldness (see photograph page 38). Perhaps this is why the Guanches chose it as their holy mountain.

At the other end of this plain lies the pleasant country village of **La Oliva**★ (87km ⬩✕). It rests on the edge of a lava flow. Montaña Arena, a mountain of sand, rises up out of the lava flow in the background. La Oliva was a town of some importance in the 17th century, when the island's military post was stationed here. The official residence (the colonels' house; sketch page 6) can be seen abandoned on the outskirts of the village, on your right, as you enter. Legend has it that it contains 365 doors and windows. To the left of the building stand the rustic servants' quarters and stables. One can't help but notice the perfectly-shaped Montaña Frontón rising up in the background of this naked setting; in fact, it's not a real mountain, but only the tail of a long ridge. The parish church at La Oliva, Nuestra Señora de Candelaria, overpowers the village with its solid black-stone belfry. The Casa del Capellán (chaplain's house), another old and dilapidated building, sits off the side of the Corralejo road, on the left. This house, and a small house in the village, which has a stone façade with an Aztec motif, are other examples of the as yet unexplained Mexican influence (see also Tour 1, Pájara).

From La Oliva you can take an alternative route home another day, via Caldereta: head east for the coast and keep left at the first junction (see the touring map). This quiet little village has some excellent examples of traditional architecture, from simple farm dwellings to comfortable villas. But today's tour leaves La Oliva for Lajares: take the road forking off left opposite the church (not signposted). The road runs alongside the pale green lichen-smeared *malpais* (the 'badlands') — a pleasant change in the landscape. We circle Montaña La Arena before coming into **Lajares** (96km) and passing between two roadside windmills. The one on our left is called a *molina*: a wooden contraption that rotates and is built onto the rooftop of a house. The house normally has a room on either side of the mill. On our right we have a *molino*: it's conical and is moved by pushing the long arms, thus moving the cap with the windmill blades. This building is not inhabited. Both mills were used for grinding *gofio*. See sketches on pages 1 and 2. Lajares is an attractive little village of white houses set amidst dark lava-stone walls.

We follow the lava flow all the way to **El Cotillo** (103km ♠✕), at present just a jumble of houses set around a pretty rocky port. Make the most of it now; the speculators have found another stupendous stretch of coast to develop. A superb beach set below cliffs lies over to the left of the village. Take any of the tracks leading out past the 17th-century watchtower — Castillo de Rico Roque (🏛), perched on the cliffs at the edge of the village. You will find exquisite little coves ensconced in the dark lava coastline (***Picnic 2***; photograph page 37).

When you call it a day, the homeward-bound route is straightforward. Keep straight on (left) through Lajares and, at the GC600, keep left for Corralejo.

In spring patches of scarlet poppies light up the countryside. The windmill in the background is used for drawing water from sunken wells (see notes on page 16).

1 AROUND LOBOS

Distance: 10km/6.2mi; 1h45min

Grade: easy, but there is no shade, and it can be hot, windy and dusty.

Equipment: comfortable shoes, cardigan, sunhat, suncream, picnic, plenty of water, swimwear

How to get there: ⛴ from Corralejo to Lobos
Departs Corralejo at 10.00 daily
To return: same ⛴ from Lobos; departs 16.00 daily

You can have Jandía and El Jable; I'll settle for Lobos any day. A 35-minute — and not too rough — ferry ride with an amiable seafarer takes you over to this strange little island of sand and rocky mounds. Seen from Corralejo, it may not even arouse your curiosity. But once you've seen the exquisite lagoon cradled by Casas El Puertito and you've climbed the crater, then finished your day with a dip in the turquoise green waters off the shore, you'll remember it as one of the most beautiful spots on Fuerteventura. Lobos takes its name from the seals that once inhabited these waters. The island is only 3km off the coast of Fuerteventura and measures 6.5km square.

We follow a track that circles the island. No one lives on Lobos, so there are no vehicles. Straight off the jetty, **start out** by taking the right-hand fork and head for the tiny port of Casas El Puertito, a few minutes away. A neat wide path leads us through a landscape dominated by mounds of lava and littered with rock. These small mounds, called *hornitos* ('little ovens'; see page 32) are caused by phreatic eruptions. You'll see the very beautiful *Limonium papillatum*, with its paper-like mauve and white flowers. And fluorescent green *tabaiba* glows amidst the sombre rock. You'll also notice plenty of *cosco* (*Mesembryanthemum nodiflorum*; see page 40), a noticeably bright, reddish plant, and *Suaeda vera.*

A reef of rocky outcrops shelters the lagoon, making it into a perfect natural swimming pool. Through the rock you can see the sand dunes of Corralejo in the background; this is a picture postcard setting. Exiting from the little houses, we continue around the lagoon. Almost at once, swing back inland and come to a T-junction: keep left here. *Arthrocnemum fruticosum* (a fern-like plant) grows in the hollows. Ice plants, with their transparent papillae resembling drops of water, may also catch your attention. This plant was once traded for its soda content. The track loops its way through these miniature 'mountains'. Small sandy depressions lie ensconced amidst them. The rock is clad in orange and faded-green lichen.

Overlooking all this is Montaña Lobos (the crater), the most prominent feature in this natural park.

Shortly, cross a sandy flat area. The track forks; the right-hand fork becomes a path and cuts off a couple of corners and rejoins the main route on the top of a bank. Lanzarote begins to grow across the horizon. Ignore the forks off to the right at **15min** and **20min** into the walk. The second fork leads past a patch of *sisal* — an aloe-like plant with exceptionally tall flower stems, sheltering in a hollow just two minutes away. Close on **30min** into the walk, you come to a faint T-junction. Bear left and, minutes further along, join a track from the left, just below the lighthouse. Then climb up to it on a paved way. In two minutes you're alongside the abandoned building and its outhouses. If you don't intend to climb the crater, this will be your best viewpoint in the walk. You look out over the dark lava hills and the tiny valleys of golden sand that thread their way through them. To the right of the broken-away crater of Montaña Lobos you'll glimpse Corralejo. Across the straits lie Lanzarote's magnificent beaches, stretching from Playa Blanca to Punta Papagayo (just opposite you).

From the lighthouse we follow the main track off to the right, into a manicured landscape. Just over fifteen minutes from the lighthouse (at about **55min**), we turn off to climb Montaña Lobos. Take the first (faint) fork-off you come to, on your right. Straight into this track, the route forks. Go right and, some 115 paces along this fading fork, head straight off across the stones, aiming for the path that ascends the crater. Within two minutes, cross a sandy hollow and reach the rim of the crater at about **1h05min**.

A brilliant sight awaits you. You find yourself on a razor-sharp ridge, looking down sheer walls onto a beach, hidden inside this half-crater. Your vista encompasses the profusion of *hornitos* that make up this island, the dunes of Corralejo, and the hazy inland hills. To the north, you can see all along the coastline of Lanzarote, as far as Puerto del Carmen.

Returning to the main track, head right. Barely ten minutes after joining the track, we pass behind the beach without noticing it. The turn-off to the beach lies two minutes beyond a fisherman's cottage that sits in a hollow on your left. The exquisite bay is actually a shallow lagoon that curves back deeply into the coastline. Here's where you'll end up passing the rest of the day, no doubt. Don't forget that the boat leaves at 4pm! To return to the ferry, just continue along the track.

The 'hornitos' of Lobos — an intriguing landscape

2 EL COTILLO • CASAS DE MAJANICHO • CORRALEJO

Distance: 22km/13.5mi; 3h45min

Grade: easy but long. Note that it can be *very* hot; also windy and dusty.

Equipment: comfortable shoes, cardigan, sunhat, suncream, raingear, swimwear, picnic, pleny of water

How to get there: 🚐 from Puerto del Rosario to El Cotillo (via Corralejo)

To return: taxi from Corralejo to Puerto del Rosario (or bus on the *following* day, if you spend the night at Corralejo)

Short walk: El Cotillo—Cortijo de la Costilla—El Cotillo: easy; 2h30min. Take bus as main walk; return by taxi. You can shorten this walk by another 30 minutes if you have a car: Drive almost as far as the lighthouse and leave your vehicle by the turn-off point (alongside an old water cistern on your right). However, due to the number of car break-ins, it would be wiser to leave it in the village or at one of the more popular coves en route.

Beyond the ramshackle fishing village of El Cotillo you pass superb little *playas* — white sand coves and limpid turquoise waters embraced by dark jagged arms of lava. With civilisation behind you, you head into a no-man's land, crossing a vast sea-plain and at times floundering through dunes or through rough seas of lava. Wherever you look, there are stones and rock and plains stretching for miles in all directions. But just when you're getting tired, another alluring cove appears. Time this hike for the early afternoon, when you can take dips in the numerous coves at the start of the walk and cross the inhospitable sea-plain in the cool of the evening.*

Leave the bus just inside El Cotillo, outside Supermercado El Cotillo. **Start out** by walking a few metres back to the gravel road the bus has just turned off, and bear left along it, making

*Note: The entire course of this walk can be done in a jeep, since it follows a track. But don't attempt it in your rented *car,* it's very rough in places. Remember the wording of your car-hire contract: no venturing off sealed roads is covered by insurance! *Note also:* A highly recommended bicycle excursion of 28km follows the route Corralejo—Casas de Majanicho—Lajares—Corralejo. The first 8.5km is on a bumpy dirt track. Avoid cycling on windy days! Cycles are available for rent in Corralejo.

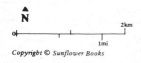

Caleta de Beatriz

Caleta de Punta Aguada

Punta de Tostón

Faro de Tostón

P

Urbanización
Los Lagos

*Playa
de Marfolin*

Corralejos →

COTILLO

■ Castillo de Rico Roque

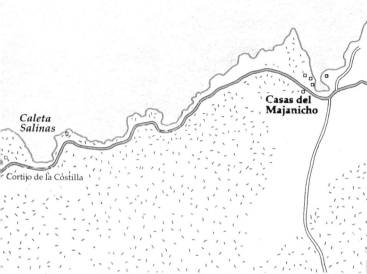

for *el faro* — the lighthouse. An *urbanización* is under way on the outskirts of El Cotillo, so the description of the first kilometre or two of this walk may change by the time you use the book. Keep straight through the new housing development, crossing a flat and sandy landscape. The way continues to the lighthouse (Faro de Tostón). Some tempting coves come out of hiding. Can you resist them? The vivid colours of the sea, the sand, and the lava around here could sell anyone on a Fuerteventura holiday.

It's quite on the cards that you will be walking into a strong wind. Reefs of rock shelter small lagoons. The red and white-striped lighthouse is the only landmark in this flat countryside. Inland, however, high hills run along the horizon. The salt-white dunes glare in the sun.

At about **30min** into the walk, not long before reaching the lighthouse, we turn off the road onto a faint sandy track veering off right. An old water cistern marks the spot. Before you lies an alluring seascape of bright coves snuggled into the jagged shore, with warm white dunes rolling back off them. These little beaches are never crowded.

Some fifteen minutes off the road we join a track coming from the right, to discover *malpais* ('badland') lava creeping in on us. This 'AA'-type lava is speckled with orange and grey-green lichen. Rock layers the ground, leaving not even a breathing space. The sand is sprinkled

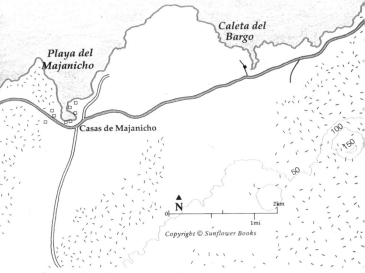

with small yellow flowers (*Tabaceae ononis*). Shortly we pass through a stone wall that fences off the dunes and cross a corner of the *malpais*. Ignore the faint fork-off left immediately through the wall. (You will remain on the main track all the way to Corralejo.) Dropping into a dusty flat, the track branches off in all directions. Head across towards the sea, bearing right, and pick up the track again as it re-enters the sand.

Looking across the *malpais* one is surprised to find that it is all fenced off by walls and well clothed in greenery. At the **1h15min**-mark we mount a gentle rise to find a fishermen's outpost consisting of a few sheds and houses — Cortijo de la Costilla. It rests on the edge of the lava, around an inlet. One of the little houses even sports a television aerial! On hazeless days you can see Lanzarote just across the straights. Midway along the track swings inland and, further along the coast, dozens of windsurfers can be seen zipping across the sea. Gradually Casas de Majanicho introduces itself. This collection of beach shacks and a couple of houses is plonked around another deeply-set inlet. The windsurfing takes place to the right of this settlement — it's one of the 'in' places.

At just over **2h** en route come to a junction, behind the houses. Continue straight on. (A right turn would take you out onto the main Cotillo road.) The way now becomes an earthen track/road. Playa Blanca is the splash of white

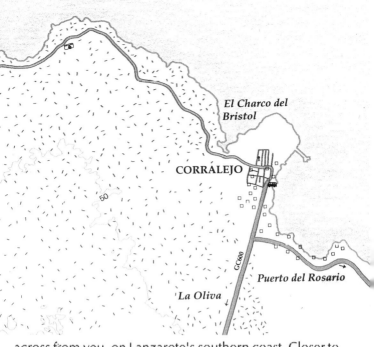

across from you, on Lanzarote's southern coast. Closer to Corralejo, the 'pimply' islet of Lobos (Walk 1) comes into sight, with its prominent crater sharply outlined. At **3h30min** we enter Corralejo from the rear, join a track coming in from the right, and head straight down (notice the old windmill here on your left) into the resort. Minutes down, swing up right to the centre. If you're staying the night here, you'll find your bus tomorrow outside the Centro Atlántico; it leaves for Puerto del Rosario at 07.30 (weekdays) or 07.45 (Sundays).

Setting off across the dunes, we look back onto the Faro de Tostón.

3 MONTAÑA TINDAYA

Distance: 6km/3.8mi; 1h15min

Grade: a strenuous, but short, ascent of 220m/720ft up a very steep, rocky mountain. This hike is difficult for inexperienced walkers and would be dangerous in wet weather.

Equipment: walking boots with good grip and ankle support, cardigan, sunhat, suncream, raingear, picnic, plenty of water

How to get there: Corralejo-🚐 or Puerto del Rosario-🚐 to Tindaya; alight at the junction above the village.

To return: 🚐 from Tindaya to Corralejo, or taxi to Puerto del Rosario (arrange for a taxi beforehand, or telephone from the restaurant below the junction).

Montaña Tindaya is no ordinary mountain. Not only is it a prominent feature in the landscape, but the Guanches regarded it as their holy mountain. On its summit they slaughtered young goats and offered these sacrifices to their gods. A number of important relics from the Guanche epoch have been found on the mountain, and rock engravings such as those on page 40 can still be seen around the summit.

Barley fields sprinkled with poppies encircle Montaña Tindaya (Walk 3, Car tour 3).

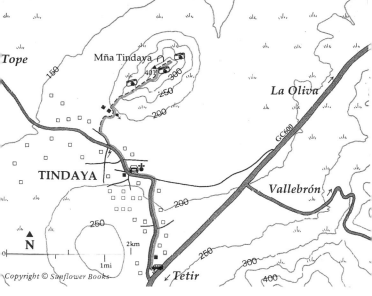

Off the bus, **start out** by following the road down into the village. Go to the church square (also the best place to leave a hired car). This peaceful farming settlement curves around the gentle slopes of a sprawling hill. The houses are scattered amidst garden plots, which sit behind the tired stone walls criss-crossing the inclines. Goats and sheep doze in their pens. Here on Fuerteventura the goats are quite a breed. Some nannies are able to give as many as 8 litres of milk over a 24-hour period! Past the church, the road curves around to the right. Now Montaña Tindaya stands before you; its sheer inclines make the summit appear inaccessible.

Five minutes beyond the church (some 60m/yds along from an electricity transformer station on your left), a small farm track forks off to the right. Take it but, a minute in, fork off onto a fainter track ascending to the right, into fields of barley. When the track fizzles out a minute further on, head up to the two derelict stone cottages in front of you (at the base of the hill). Your ascent begins just behind them, where you climb the tail of the ridge. The ground is stony and carpeted in wine-coloured *cosco* (see page 40) and ice plants. When food was scarce in years gone by, the dried fruit of the *cosco* plant was used to make an ersatz *gofio* (an important food source on the island, usually made from roasted corn). The fallen fruit of the *cosco* was collected and ground into powder.

Your way up is very straightforward: stick to the top of the crest all the way. Above the gravel you come onto bare rock. In places you'll be down on all fours.

At about **40min** you reach the summit. (The crest topples off onto the plains below some three to four minutes further on, so take care!) You have a fine view of the surrounding countryside. On clear days you can see Lanzarote — El Cotillo is the village ensconced in the coastline over on the left, and La Oliva is the sprinkling of white straight ahead off the end of the mountain. Immediately below, on the left-hand side of the mountain, sits a picturesque homestead surrounded by gardens and a lean palm grove — a pretty picture in this harsh landscape. Two minutes beyond the summit, notice the cave-like shelter set in the hillside just below on your left. This is a good place to seek shade if you've the courage to slide down the mountain face and you don't mind an enormous boulder sitting over your head....

Now for the treasure hunt. Most of the drawings/engravings are around the summit. The easiest to find are the two on an upright, smooth rock face just below the summit (on the eastern, or village side). The engravings are within a radius of some 5 to 8 metres (15 to 25 feet) from the top of the peak. Others are located on the next clump of rock further along the ridge. Once you've found one, you soon find the others. The diagrams help you to identify them. *Suerte!*

Descending the mountain is slow going. A lot of care is needed. Allow yourself enough time to return to the bus, if you didn't come by car.

A herdsman watering his goats at a small tank near the base of Montaña Tindaya. Notice the deep red cosco in the foreground.

4 LLANOS DE LA CONCEPCION • EMBALSE DE LOS MOLINOS • MORRO DE LA CUEVA • LLANOS DE LA CONCEPCION

Distance: 13km/8mi; 2h15min

Grade: moderate. Much of the walk is freewheeling over stony terrain. It can be very hot, and there is no shade beyond the reservoir.

Equipment: walking boots or stout shoes with ankle support, cardigan, sunhat, suncream, raingear, picnic, plenty of water

How to get there and return: only accessible by private transport

The Embalse de los Molinos is the largest reservoir on Fuerteventura. Its water level varies from year to year. Seeing a body of water in this dry and barren landscape is indeed a strange sight and, from the hilltops above, it makes quite a picture. Heading home, you mingle with goats and sheep, as you traipse over rolling ridges with grand views over this desolate countryside.

Leave your transport outside Bar García in Llanos de la Concepción. **Setting out**, take the track that runs down into the village from the bar. This scattering of houses is deep in slumber. Most of the garden plots are untended and overgrown. The walls no longer stand proud and straight. Notice the earthen oven on the left-hand side of the track a couple of minutes down. Clumps of prickly-pear and a few thick-leafed aloes sit behind the tired walls. Pass through an intersection and, two minutes further on, when the track forks (outside a shop), keep straight on — to the right. Another track joins you from the left a few minutes later. This is followed by a streambed crossing.

We head across a vast valley, its left side lined by smooth worn hills and its right side bordered by *cuchillos* (Spanish for 'knives': these are younger and sharper hills). The terrain is stony and dry. Solitary cultivated corners make a sharp contrast in this ochre-coloured landscape, with their vivid greenery. In spring scarlet poppies and daisies run amok in the gardens, and the plain is smeared with the cereal-like *Gramineae*. Within **15min** pass through another intersection, keeping straight on. A few lone houses seek solitude in this great expanse of open country.

Approaching the **30min**-mark we again re-enter the streambed, just as it joins another from the right. Metres (yards) along we leave it and the main track as well, ascending a faint fork-off to the left. An abandoned farmstead lies up ahead. The *barranco* begins folding up, and it's still dry. When the way swings up to the farmhouse, you continue straight off it, following the

41

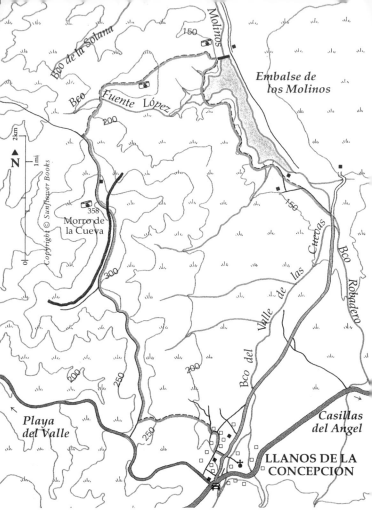

barranco. Soon the streambed opens up, revealing a river of tamarisk shrubs — the only shrubs in this countryside. They shelter here along the damp valley floor. Briefly join a two-wheeled track and cross through a dense colony of ice plants and *cosco*. You catch sight of the dam wall up ahead and gradually the tail of water below grows into a good-sized muddy brown reservoir. If you're into ornithology, go quietly: birds do congregate around the muddy end of the dam here. These tamarisk offer the only shade you'll find on the route of this walk, so it's a good picnic spot on a hot day … if you'll pardon the flies.

Continuing around the *presa*, you'll need to scramble up the rocky slopes and make your way around the inclines above the reservoir — one of the most attractive spots on the walk, where *Asphodelus* covers the slopes.

An arm of water in a small side-*barranco* needs skirting. This is also a good spot for bird-watching, and you may spot some herons. Keep around the edge of the arm of water and then ascend the side of the ridge. Descending onto the wall of the dam needs careful footwork; the hillside is steep and gravelly. You reach the wall at about **1h**. From there scramble up onto the top of the crest above the dam: from here you'll have a good vista over the reservoir and across the valley to the impressive barrier of hills. A small village (Colonia García Escamez) of white block houses lies near the end of the valley. Red *cosco* stains the surrounding inclines, and a hint of green lies in the sheltered folds. The serenity and isolation of this landscape has a beauty all its own.

Home is now over the hills we've just circled. Landmarks to aim for are (with your back to the reservoir): the hilltop immediately above, from where you curve round to the hills over on your left — heading for the stone wall that crosses over them. The timing of this leg of the walk will depend on how quickly you want to reach that summit. Once you've come to the first hilltop, descend briefly to your right, before crossing the streambed below on your left. The beauty of freewheeling on these low hills is that it's just about impossible to get lost.

At about **1h20min** cross the streambed that runs between the two ridges. Mounting an adjoining ridge, you come onto a faint two-wheeled track and look straight out over another valley. Pass a stone shelter near the top of the crest and soon the coast comes into view on your right. Close on **1h40min** into the walk you reach the second hilltop (Morro de la Cueva) and the highest point in the walk (363m/1190ft) — near the 'Great Wall' of Llanos de la Concepción (an impressive stretch of wall along the top of the ridge). On these slopes you'll encounter a rather comical-looking flock of sheep grazing. Inland lie bare desiccated hills, climbing one upon the other.

Remaining on the track, pass through the wall and follow it all along the top of the ridge. Llanos de la Concepción is now in sight below you. Valle de Santa Inés huddles high in the hills. Ten minutes through the walls, our track swings up onto a lateral ridge branching off left (towards the village). The wall and a faint fork continue to the right. More of Santa Inés opens up, and terracing, stepping shallow *barrancos*, comes out of hiding.

Descending to the village, we pass by two rubbish dumps (hopefully the expected upsurge in tourism to the

Embalse de los Molinos, Fuerteventura's largest reservoir — and a good spot for birdwatching. The surrounding countryside is silent and barren.

island will elicit some action on the part of the government to get rid of Fuerteventura's many unsightly rubbish dumps...). Just past the second dump, some fifteen minutes down (not far off a road), leave the track and descend to the village on a goats' path. Rounding the crest, our path quickly fades out. Then we flounder over loose stones and gravel, before coming into the village.

Descending the hill, keep the church on your left and find a farm track at the bottom of the stone wall that runs down on your right. Follow this track to a gravel driveway. Almost immediately you'll join a track from the left and, two minutes later, take the first turn-off left. This takes you down onto the track you set off along at the start of the walk — the intersection above the church. Bear right and, in three minutes, at **2h15min**, you're back at the bar (open from 5.30 or 6.00 pm) all ready for a beer....

5 BARRANCO DE LAS PEÑITAS (VEGA DE RIO DE PALMAS)

Distance: 5km/3mi; 1h30min   **See also photograph page 25**

Grade: quite easy, but the path to the chapel could prove unnerving for those prone to vertigo. Be very careful if it's wet!

Equipment: comfortable shoes or walking boots, cardigan, sunhat, suncream, raingear, picnic, plenty of water

How to get there and return: only accessible by private transport

This stroll is short and sweet; it takes us down one of the island's most picturesque valleys, the Barranco de las Peñitas. Palm trees dot the valley, and a small reservoir rests in the floor. From the reservoir wall you look through a corridor of rock out onto more palms and salubrious garden plots far below. In winter you may find dark green pools embedded in the floor of the *barranco*. Hidden in the sheer walls lies the delightful little Ermita de Nuestra Señora de la Peña — just the kind of place where one might feel inclined to offer up a prayer.

To reach the **starting point** of the walk, turn off the GC620 (approaching from Pajara) just before the centre of Vega de Río de Palmas and drive down towards the reservoir. The safest place to leave your car is probably just past the school building, half a kilometre downhill, on your left. For the first five minutes of the walk we follow the road, passing the last of the houses. A healthy sprinkling of tall palms graces the valley floor and indeed, the entire valley. For Fuerteventura, this is the height of arboreal luxury! Abrupt craggy ridges dominate the landscape.

We turn off from the road onto a wide goats' path; this heads off to the right, just before a culvert and bridge. The goats' path follows the streambed. A minute along we drop down into it (just to the right of a stone embankment crossing the *barranco*). Some ten minutes below the bridge (**15min**) we come to clumps of tamarisk in the middle of the streambed. Here we climb out of the *barranco* onto an old washed-out track that ascends to the right. The valley floor quickly fills with tamarisk and then forks. The left-hand fork swings back up into the hills;

the right-hand fork cradles the reservoir, before folding up into a narrow ravine that drops down to join the Barranco de Mal Paso.

We're surrounded by hills. The pointed Gran Montaña (708m/2320ft) dominates the valley. Soon the murky green *presa* is just below you. Green garden plots set amidst palm trees terrace the slopes on your left now. Our *barranco*, barren and bouldery, is freckled with *verode* — the brightest plant on the slopes. Five minutes along, the track ends, directly above the reservoir wall. The bare escarpment stares down on us, as it closes up into a deep 'V' which empties out onto an oasis of palms and gardens before continuing its seaward journey. If you want to see more of this scenic *barranco*, head back up the track for a minute, or until you can scramble down the hillside (without ending up in the reservoir!) to the goats' path that runs along the water's edge, and head along this to the reservoir wall. Take care — it's a bit narrow!

Beyond the reservoir wall we follow a stone-paved path that has been built into the sides of the *barranco*. Parts of this path are tricky going, where it has crumbled away … and the lizards darting every which way don't help. The pools may be no more than puddles by the time you use this book, but they *can* be very deep. A few minutes down the path you spot the tiny white chapel of Nuestra Señora de la Peña perched on a rocky outcrop above the streambed. We turn off to the chapel a minute later. This path clings to the face of the rock and is quite unnerving, but it's fairly short — only some 30m/yds. Inside the chapel you'll find a 15th-century alabaster image of the island's patron saint, Our Lady of the Rock, as well as a visitor's book that makes for interesting reading. On a scorchingly-hot day, the chapel provides the perfect retreat for a picnic. Beyond the *ermita* the path hangs out over the side of the *barranco*. This stretch of path might also prove unnerving for those without a head for heights. It's

The tiny chapel of Nuestra Señora de la Peña is well concealed in a sheer ravine. Can you spot it? There's a close-up view below. Another photo of this lovely barranco is on page 25 (Picnic 5, Car tour 1).

an impressive piece of path-building, that's for certain. Nearing the end of the *barranco*, a few minutes along, the path vanishes. We call it quits here, **40min** after setting out. This is a very picturesque corner of the valley, where you look out over gardens and the on-going ravine.

Returning, we follow the same route but, instead of climbing to the track above the reservoir, we remain on the goats' path, keeping around the hillside until we re-enter the streambed just above the reservoir. There's quite a bit of bird life near the water's edge; keep your eyes peeled!

Picnic 5: The chapel of Nuestra Señora de la Peña in the Peñitas barranco. Fine pools like these are a rarity on Fuerteventura!

6 PUERTO DE LA PEÑA • BARRANCO DE LA MADRE DEL AGUA • PEÑA HORADADA • PUERTO DE LA PEÑA

Distance: 12km/7.5mi; 2h15min

Grade: moderate. The beginning of the walk is awkward and involves some scrambling; however, it is not difficult. The ascent in the rocky bed of the Barranco de la Madre del Agua will be slow. Getting into the cave at the end of the hike requires sure-footedness and a head for heights, and should only be attempted by very experienced walkers. Don't attempt this hike in wet weather.

Equipment: comfortable shoes or walking boots, cardigan, sunhat, raingear, suncream, swimwear, picnic, plenty of water

How to get there and return: accessible by private transport only

Short walks: both are easy —
1 Puerto de la Peña—Peña Horadada—Puerto de la Peña (1h10min). Do the walk in reverse by using the notes for Picnic 6b as far as the Caleta Negra overlook; then refer to the map to continue to the Peña Horadada. Wear comfortable shoes and take swimming things. *Note:* Swim in the pool below the rock with the hole in it (see below); the beach looks potentially dangerous to me.
2 Puerto de la Peña—Barranco de la Madre del Agua—Puerto de la Peña (45min). Follow the main walk as far as Barranco de la Madre del Agua. If it appeals to you, do some exploring there.

This excursion gives you a taste of everything. It's well worth a day of your holiday. You set out seeing some of Fuerteventura's loveliest palm groves and then ascend a tiny *barranco* unique for its permanent flowing stream (don't expect a torrent, however!). Set out early in the morning, so you can see the goatherds milking their goats at a corral midway into the walk. Later in the day, we enjoy some striking coastal scenery, as we detour to the rock with a hole in it and the caves of Caleta Negra.

This monumental rock with a hole in it ('Peña Horadada') sits at the mouth of the Barranco de la Peña. The small pool beneath it is ideal for cooling off....

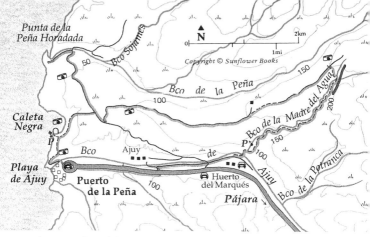

The usual problem is, where to leave the car? The safest place (but not the closest) is Puerto de la Peña, from where you can walk back up the road for ten minutes and then **begin the walk.** Just beyond an abandoned homestead across the *barranco*, see a faint track forking off the road to it, crossing a garden plot, and descending into the *barranco*. Follow this track. We head up this wide stream-bed to the right, along the track. A profusion of tamarisk trees grows along the sides of the banks; they soon broaden out into hedges and create windbreaks for the gardens. Approaching our turn-off, we pass small groves of tall palms.

The Barranco de la Madre del Agua is a discrete narrow ravine that slices its way into the ridge trailing down on our left. Palm trees peeping out of it give its presence away. A small farm sits opposite it. Less than ten minutes up the *barranco*, when the track veers off along the right-hand side of the streambed, we continue over to the left, to Madre del Agua. The initial stretch of this ravine is the most awkward part of the hike, since we have to flounder over rocks and palm fronds (watch out for these!) in the streambed. As compensation, this cool shady grove is a delightful discovery, with its murmuring little stream and clear pools. A neat stone wall lining the right-hand bank, and a charming crumbled stone bridge catch your attention through the trees (see page 51). Further ahead, the ravine floor is choked with cane. Altogether, it's a pleasant place to explore, especially on a hot day.

Once you've done some exploring, the easiest way out is to cross the bridge and ascend the right-hand wall of the ravine, scaling above a small tank just beyond the bridge. Follow the goats' path along the steep gravelly hillside, keeping above the cane. Past the cane, you re-enter the streambed just by an old and twisted tamarisk tree (five minutes from the bridge). The jungle of vegetation has vanished, and we now scramble up the rocky ravine floor. The walls rise straight up above us. Depending on the rains, small *charcos* (pools) lie at intervals; beyond the cane the stream is subterranean and only occasionally resurfaces. A couple of pools may require tricky footwork. *Asphodelus* and the stringy tobacco plant shrub (*Nicotiana glauca*) are the sole survivors up here. It's a most inhospitable landscape, where only goats can forage. Still, you may see some birds up here.

Some **25min** of twisting and turning brings you to a small *barranco* forking off left from the main ravine. An old stone wall climbs out of the streambed to the left just at this point. Here we also scramble out of the streambed and ascend to the crest above; this is easiest done by climbing the left-hand side of the *barranco*. Three minutes up (at about **50min** into the walk) we find ourselves on the well-rounded top of a crest, where we find a faint track. Half a minute across the crest, we look down into a much grander *barranco* — the Barranco de la Peña, which may also carry a trickle of water. Smooth, rounded hills, bare of life, grow up in the background.

At the mouth of the Barranco de la Madre del Agua — the site of a permanently-flowing stream. Here you can enjoy Picnic 6a, under a profusion of palms.

Continuing down the stony track, pass the crumbled remains of an old corral. In the distance, to the left, you can see the village of Mezguez, noticeable for its grassy surroundings. At just over **1h** you pass (quietly, please) a large corral. This is the home of a handsome herd of goats and a number of sheep. The animals are milked in the morning, then turned out to graze. Please note — the family here is reserved and not used to intruders. So don't interrupt their privacy, unless they invite you over, and do ask for permission before taking any photographs ("Por favor" — pointing to your camera). Watching the herd at play is very amusing. The dogs are noisy and harmless.

From the corral you follow a clear track downhill. The coast begins to appear, and you catch a glimpse of Puerto de la Peña, a small gathering of modest houses set back off the sea. Twenty minutes below the corral come to a junction. Keep right. A minute along, pass a fork-off left: this is your return route. Dipping to the sea, the majestic Peña Horadada (the 'rock with a hole in it') dramatically appears. This massive 'Arc de Triomphe' of rock thrusts up off the beach at the water's edge. We descend now into the Barranco de la Peña, over which we looked earlier.

Close on **1h35min** you're standing below the great gaping hole, dwarfed by this monumental wall of rock. A splendid little pool, which the waves replenish, sits below the hole. The coastline is wild and very beautiful. If you plan to swim, please use the pool; the beach is dangerous.

We follow the same track out, but turn off it some ten minutes along. Take the faint fork to the right (mentioned earlier) that heads towards the top of the cliffs. Minutes along, when the way ends, bear left and, a minute later, you're on the edge of the cliffs with a magnificent view around Caleta Negra. The caves you see cutting back into the walls over on the left can be reached by following the steps down to the old pier. Three minutes around the cliffs bring you to the descending point (steps). *Note: this descent is only recommended for very experienced and sure-footed walkers; you'll have to scramble some 2m/6ft down to the steps (the top steps are washed away) — on all fours, and with the sea thrashing around directly below you. Don't venture down to the caves if the sea is rough!* A goats' path leads down to the steps, which are to the left of the stone wall lodged in the face of the hill just below the top of the crest. Two minutes down, you're overlooking the pier and a minute later you're on the sandy floor of the first massive cavern. Another, narrower cave reaches to within 50 metres/yards of Puerto de la Peña! But please — just take my word for it and remain in the main chamber. Don't go exploring!

Now making for Puerto de la Peña, continue around the top of the crest and in two minutes overlook the village and its black sand beach. Head along the crest to the point on your right and scramble down to the old path to the pier. Follow it into the village(**2h10min).**

7 PICO DE LA ZARZA

Distance: 16km/10mi; 3h15min   **Photograph opposite**

Grade: strenuous, with an ascent of 807m/2650ft. The first 75 minutes of the walk follows a track, but then you must clamber over rocks and stones for about 20 minutes more to reach the summit. It can be very hot — or very cold and windy. Not recommended on very windy days — nor on cloudy days, since the climb is only worth it for the view and, if you were lost in mist, the climb could be dangerous as well. But everyone who is fit should try this hike, beginners included.

Equipment: walking boots or stout shoes with ankle support, warm jacket, raingear, sunhat (and something with which to tie it to your head!), suncream, picnic, plenty of water

How to get there and return: with your own rented car, or by taxi to the Hotel Río Ventura in the Barranco de Vinamar

P ico de la Zarza is Fuerteventura's highest peak and worth climbing for two reasons: the grand panorama that tumbles away below you and the wealth of botanical specimens to be seen en route. The best time to scale this mountain is in spring, when the summit is resplendent with yellow-flowering *Asteriscus* (see opposite). But, be warned: it can be *very* windy! On a calm day, it's one of the most exhilarating spots on the island.

The **departing point** for the walk is in the Barranco de Vinamar, just outside the village of Morro del Jable. Hotel Río Ventura and Apartamentos Río Maxorata sit on the right-hand side of the mouth of this *barranco*. Take the road up alongside the apartments, following the streambed and, three minutes up, turn off to the right to climb to the Hotel Río Ventura. Our track begins behind this hotel. (It is very likely that future construction will change the layout of this area, but the start of the walk should be easy to locate from this hotel.) Look for the track that climbs above the hotel and follow it all the way up the ridge. Initially the way curves round the hillside to the right, before it strikes off left up the nose of the ridge. A few minutes from the hotel we fork off left and begin the ascent to the peak along a rough and rocky track. A stiff climb lies ahead, but already we have a superb view back over the long white Playa del Matorral with its turquoise-green shoreline. The Barranco de Vinamar, as bleak as the rest of the countryside, cuts straight back into the massif.

Climbing higher, you catch sight of corrals hidden in the depths of the ravine. On rounding to the right-hand side of the ridge, you overlook another harsh valley,

Opposite: From atop Pico de la Zarza — the island's highest peak — you have an eagle's-eye view along the isolated west coast of the Jandía Peninsula. Walk 8 takes you to the stunning beaches of the west.

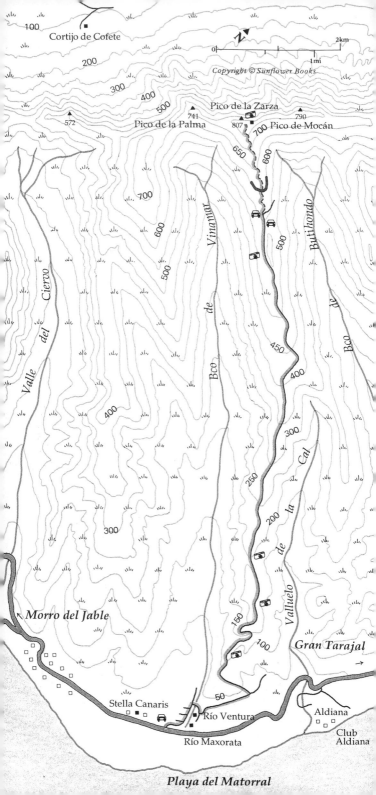

where more ridges hint at a succession of ravines in the distance. Pico de la Zarza is the unimpressive mountain-top that rises a thumbnail above the rest of the massif at the very end of this ridge. Reaching the cloud zone, you discover that the top of the crest is very herbaceous. It's quite a wild garden! Keep well clear of any goats you might encounter up here; they are *very* easily frightened and will dart off in all directions if startled. In particular, avoid any with kids. Just before the track ends, and the final assault, you head alongside a bouldery crest, flooded with *tabaiba* bushes. Look, too, onto the walls below you, to spot some enormous *candelabra*.

The track ends at about **1h15min** into the walk (at the second parking space). The remains of an unused track *do* continue off around the hillside to the right, but we do not: we head straight up to the crest of the ridge, following goats' paths to the summit. Aim for the poles and hut on the peak and take your time. The small piles of stones just serve to confuse you, so ignore them. *Lamarzkia aurea* (it resembles a bottle-brush) flourishes up here. Soon the slopes are ablaze with golden yellow flowers: *Asteriscus*, a pretty furry green-leafed plant.

At **1h35min**, windswept and exhausted, you're on the roof of the island. And what a view! To the left you look across the lofty crags that rupture this impenetrable wall of rock. The jutting southwestern coastline unfolds as this barrier of mountains dies down into sand-patched hills and finally a sea-plain. Don't venture too near to the edge of the peak; it plummets hundreds of feet straight down onto a sea-flat. A mysterious European-style mansion with a turret sits back off the flat in the shadows of the cliffs. This is the Cortijo de Cofete (see Walk 8). More in keeping with the landscape is Cofete, the hamlet of small huts over to the left. To your right stand the high rolling sand hills of the Pared isthmus that joins these mountains to the northern half of the island. On hazeless days you see well down the eastern coastline to Lanzarote in the distance.

Botanists will want to tarry here on the summit for quite some time to discover more of the island's floral treasures: *Echium handiense, Bupleurum handiense, Sideritis massoniana, Argyranthemum winteri,* and the more common *Ranunculus cortusifolius, Andryala cheiranthifolia, Minuartia platyphylla,* and *orobanche.* The summit also houses a tiny meteorological hut.

Home is all downhill — sheer bliss — some hour and a half's descent away.

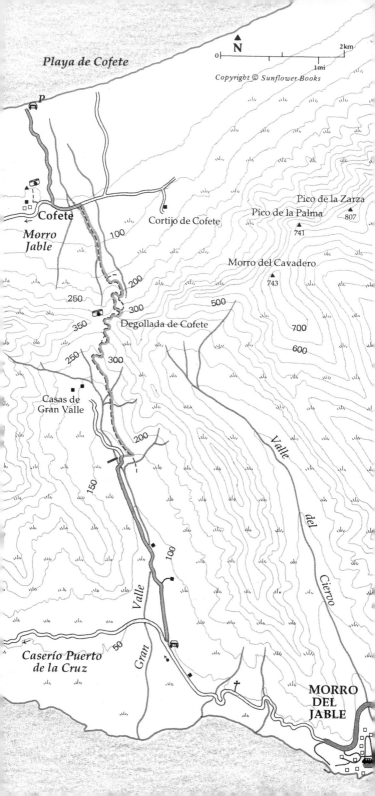

Playa de Cofete

0 | N | 2km
1mi

Copyright © Sunflower Books

P

Cofete

Morro Jable

Cortijo de Cofete

Pico de la Zarza
▲ 807

Pico de la Palma
▲ 741

100

200

Morro del Cavadero
▲ 743

250

300

Degollada de Cofete

500

350

250

300

700

600

Casas de
Gran Valle

200

Valle

150

del

100

Cierro

Valle

50

Caserío Puerto
de la Cruz

Gran

†

MORRO
DEL
JABLE

8 BARRANCO GRAN VALLE • DEGOLLADA DE COFETE • PLAYA DE COFETE • BARRANCO GRAN VALLE

Distance: 15km/9.2mi; 3h   **Map opposite; photograph page 23**

Grade: strenuous. The pass (Degollada de Cofete) costs you a 300m/985ft climb — *twice*. The path on the west coast is rocky and stony. There is some free-wheeling over rocky terrain. It can be very hot, and there is no shade en route. The walk is only recommended for sure-footed experienced hikers with a head for heights.

Equipment: walking boots, warm cardigan, sunhat, raingear, suncream, swimwear, picnic, as much water as you can possibly manage to carry

How to get there and return: use your own transport, or take a taxi to the fork-off up into the Barranco Gran Valle. If the driver doesn't know where it is, it is the ravine beyond Morro del Jable, less than 5km out of the village. Don't forget to ask the driver to return for you!

C ross the Jandía Peninsula to the isolated west coast and see what isolated *really* means! From the crest of the *cumbre* you will have magnificent sweeping views along the beaches of Cofete and Barlovento de Jandía. The empty beaches and crashing breakers are enough to send anyone running down to meet them. Make sure you're fit enough to tackle this hike, however! You may also see the *burros salvajes* — the wild donkeys that roam these hills (twelve of them at the last count, so I'm told). They apparently sneak down to ravage the gardens under cover of night.

A water tank on the left-hand side of the road, just before the Barranco Gran Valle track, is a good landmark for the fork-off into the ravine, where the **walk begins**, 4.5km from Morro del Jable. Standing at the entrance to this austere *barranco,* you can see all the way to the end of it. An abandoned settlement of stone corrals shelters at the foot of the lofty summits. On either side of you the valley floor sweeps back up into severe rocky walls. Out here you meet only goats. Setting off up the track, keep an eye out for the rare cactus-like *Euphorbia handicnse* off the side of the track (see page 23). There is quite a colony of it here, and it only grows in a few places south of Morro del Jable. The only other vegetation in this stony terrain is the tobacco plant, *cosco, Lycium intricatum,* and *aulaga.*

Some **5min** along, reach a corral of some substance, with pens constructed out of everything from fishing nets to tin, and anything else they may have scavenged. It even boasts a TV aerial. Keeping left, descend into the streambed, and remain in it until you come to an earthen dam wall with a gaping hole in it (**10min** en route). Here the track swings across in front of the dam, circling it, and then re-enters the *barranco*. Above the dam wall, on your right, you'll see a wide path heading along the hillside. Climb up to it and continue further into the valley. Soon you look out onto the tired stone pens of Casas de Gran Valle, the old pastoral outpost you could see from the outset of the walk. You cross a couple of dry side-streams before the real ascent begins. The path fades now and again, but remains easy to follow.

At the foot of the pass the way swings back to the right to begin a 'Z'. The goats have taken a short-cut and head straight up; we follow them and rejoin the path two minutes up. Small piles of stones help mark the route. This path is now used very seldomly and has crumbled away in parts, but in the past it was the main east—west route across the peninsula. Notice the *Lamarzkia aurea*, the grassy plant flanking the way. Nearing the col, you cross a colourful rock-face bare of vegetation, and the way fades out. Keep to the right-hand side of the pass.

Crossing the pass (Degollada de Cofete), you look up at towering crags that stand like sentries on either side of you. Montaña Fraile is the sharp, pointed peak on the left. Stretching out below you are the striking golden beaches of Cofete (left) and Barlovento de Jandía (right). A chateau-type villa with a turret (so obviously out of place in this bleak landscape) immediately captures your attention. Stories abound about this amazing house, and it still remains shrouded in mystery. It belonged until recently to a Sr Winter, a German who has since died. He came to the island before World War II, and he owned the entire peninsula. When the house was constructed in the early '40s, he forbade his workers (or anyone, for that matter) to reside in Cofete. Everyone had to return to Morro del Jable at the end of the day. And from then on, stories have grown about the place — which would be a good setting for a Hitchcock film! Cofete is the forgotten outpost of stone and cement-block huts you see. The dazzling stretch of coastline detracts from the 'unsympathetic' surroundings.

Your continuation starts off as a good clear path on the right-hand side of the pass, but it rapidly deteriorates. The lichen-flecked pinnacles of rock that pierce this range keep drawing your attention. This chain of volcanic mountains harbours the island's most interesting flora. Five minutes below the pass, notice a faint fork-off to the left that swings down the nose of the crest. Here the main path veers to the right, but we go left to zig-zag down the ridge. It's slippery, but an easier route. Within minutes you will rejoin the main path again. Washed-out sections of the path call for sure foot-work. Not far above the sea-flat, the path crumbles away completely. Here we drop down the side of the ridge, free-wheeling amidst the rock — probably on your backside! Aim for the *barranco* running down on your left and walk down inside it (it's easier than floundering over the rock). On clear days you see the sand dunes of the Pared isthmus falling off into the sea, as well as the hills that enclose Pajara. The *riscos* (cliffs) rise up into dark, sinister shadows behind you.

Accompanied by large, but friendly, yellow grass-hoppers desporting themselves in the *Gramineae*, you will come to a track cutting across in front of you (30 minutes below the pass). Turn left on the track. Cofete certainly is an outpost. The only real 'building' is a bar/restaurant; the rest of the hamlet is a scattering of huts. Wine-red *cosco* provides the only colour in this sun-bleached countryside. Close on **1h20min** into the walk (three minutes along the track), you turn off right to the beach; it lies some ten minutes away. The road to this beach is only accessible (at present) to four-wheel-drive vehicles, which means that you usually share glorious Playa de Cofete with only a few other people. *Beware when you swim:* the water is only safe up to about waist-level; there is a terrific undertow.

Home is back the way we came, over the pass. You turn off the Cofete track at the second *barranco* crossing and head up the streambed. Approaching the ridge, bear left towards it and scramble up the hillside to the path; the rest of the return route is straightforward.

Cortijo de Cofete

✿ Index

Geographical names comprise the only entries in this index; for other entries, see Contents on page 3. **Bold-face** type indicates a photograph; *italic* type indicates a map reference.

60

STOP PRESS

IMPORTANT

We frequently receive letters from people who say that Noel Rochford's walking times are misleading. In his Walking Introduction, Noel always warns readers that he is a *'very fit, very fast walker'*. Unfortunately many people don't read the introduction. Probably one of the reasons for the fast timings is that Noel always walks alone ... just what we ask you *not* to do! *We urge all readers to compare their pace to Noel's on one or two short walks before setting out on longer hikes.*

CAR TOURS

Tour 3: Near the 'Colonels' House' at **La Oliva** is a brand-new art centre (Casa Mané) which, apart from its modern art exhibition, is of interest for its remarkable architecture.

WALKS

Scales: Sorry! The scales are incorrect on the walking maps: for '1mi' read '1km' and for '2km' read '1mi'.

Walk 2: Since the majority of visitors stay in Corralejo, consider doing this walk in reverse. You can start out earlier, have a (late) lunch at Mama María's in Cotillo, and return from there on the 17.30 bus.

Walk 5: This walk is only accessible by car. The best parking place is an open field behind the chemist's (which in turn is behind the school referred to in the text).

Walk 7: The area around the hotel Río Ventura is now fenced in, and you cannot get to the walk from the grounds of the hotel, so head directly for the peak from the road in front of the hotel... The track up to Pico Zarza is closed to vehicles at an altitude of 200m (where you may see a 'no entry' (for vehicles) sign in Spanish, and there are no longer any parking areas at 550m, as shown on the map.

BUSES

These bus departures were *valid in 1993.* There are more services than those listed in the book.

Line 1 (Puerto del Rosario/Morro Jable): departs Pto.d.R. 10.30, 13.15, 16.00, 19.00 (Mon-Fri); 10.30, 13.15, 16.00 (Sat); 10.00, 14.00, 20.30 (Sun); departs Morro Jable 06.00, 09.00, 13.30, 16.30 (Mon-Sat); 06.00, 18.00 (Sun).

Line 2 (Puerto del Rosario/Vega de Río Palma): departs Pto.d.R. 10.00, 14.00 (Mon-Sat); departs Vega d.R.P. 07.00, 12.30 (Mon-Sat); no Sunday buses.

Line 3 (Puerto del Rosario/Caleta Fuste — airport bus): departs Pto.d.R. 07.00-19.00 on the hour (daily); returns 30 minutes later.

Line 4 (Pájara/Morro Jable): departs Pajara 06.30 daily; departs Morro Jable 16.15 daily.

Line 5 (Costa Calma/Morro Jable): departs Costa Calma 11.30, 12.30, 15.30; departs Morro Jable 11.00, 12.00, 15.00 (daily).

Line 6 (Puerto del Rosario/Corralejo): departs Pto.d.R. 07.00, 09.30, 12.00, 15.00, 17.00; departs Corralejo 08.00, 11.00, 13.00, 16.00, 18.00 (daily).

Line 7 (Puerto del Rosario/Cotillo): departs Pto.d.R. 10.00, 14.00; departs Cotillo 07.00, 12.00 (daily).

Line 8 (Corralejo/Cotillo): departs Corralejo 18.00; departs Cotillo 17.30 (daily).

Line 9 (Pajara/Morro Jable): departs Pajara 06.30, 12.00; departs Morro Jable 10.00, 16.00 (daily).

FERRIES

The ferry service between the islands is much improved. Ferry Betancuria supplied the following timetable in 1993:

depart Playa Blanca (Lanzarote) 09.00, 11.00, 15.30, 18.00*
*19.00 from April to October

depart Corralejo (Fuerteventura) 08.00, 10.00 14.30, 17.00*
*18.00 from April to October